Only One Woof

James Herriot

Illustrated by Peter Barrett

© 1974, 1985 James Herriot
Illustrations © 1985 Peter Barrett
Printed in the U.S.A.
ISBN 0-312-58583-7
LCN 85-11768

St. Martin's Press.
New York

One nice thing about being a country vet is that there are so many interesting things to see when I visit the farms.

One sunny spring day, I visited Mr Wilkin's farm and I laughed as I watched the two sheepdog puppies playing together in the farmyard.

"Those two really love each other, don't they?"
I said.

Mr Wilkin nodded. "Aye, they are great friends.
They are never apart."

Mr Wilkin was a busy man, with many cows, pigs and sheep to look after, but he still had time for his favourite hobby – breeding and training sheepdogs. For many years, he had won silver cups all over the country. From the latest litter, he had picked the two best pups, Gyp and Sweep, and he was going to train them to run in the sheepdog trials.

The two little animals were rolling about in a happy wrestling match, growling and panting, chewing gently at each other's legs. Then suddenly they stopped playing as something else caught their attention.

"Look at that!" I cried in amazement. "They're behaving like grown-up dogs."

The pups were beginning to round up a group of tiny ducklings – much to the annoyance of the mother duck. With noses outstretched and stomachs nearly flat on the cobbles of the farmyard, they crept up on the ducklings.

"Yes," the farmer replied. "They are only twelve weeks old but their mother and father, their grandmothers and grandfathers, and away back as long as I can remember, were all sheepdogs. So these little things were born wanting to round up chickens, ducks, lambs – anything they see."

The two doggy friends were different in appearance.
Sweep was black and white while Gyp was black, white
and brown. But the thing you noticed most was that one of
Gyp's ears stuck up while the other ear lay flat against his
head. This gave him a funny, lop-sided look. In fact, he
looked a bit of a clown, but he was a friendly, tail-wagging
clown.

"There's one odd thing about Gyp," Mr Wilkin said.
"He's never barked at all."

I looked at him in surprise. "You mean never ever?"

"That's right, not a single bark. The other dogs make a
noise when strangers come to the farm, but I've never
heard Gyp make a sound since he was born."

I shook my head. "How very strange. I've never heard of
such a thing."

I got into my car and, as I drove away, I noticed that
while Sweep and two other farm dogs barked their
farewells loudly, Gyp merely wagged his tail and looked at
me in a friendly manner, his pink tongue lolling out of his
open mouth. A silent dog.

Some months later, just before Christmas, George Crossley, one of Mr Wilkin's oldest friends, and a very keen sheepdog trainer, came to ask if he could buy a dog as his own old dog had died. Mr Wilkin sold Sweep to him. I was a bit surprised about this because I knew that Sweep was further forward in his training than Gyp and looked like turning into a real champion. But it was Gyp he kept – perhaps it was because he just liked him. He was a funny dog with that lop-sided charm that was difficult to resist.

Gyp must have been sad to lose his brother and best friend and there was no doubt that he missed him, but there were other dogs on the farm and even if they didn't make up for Sweep, he was never really lonely. Although Gyp grew up big and strong, he wasn't quite clever enough to compete in the trials. So he just helped Mr Wilkin by herding the sheep and cattle on the farm. He was very happy to be out with his master all day, but perhaps he wondered where his doggy friend had gone.

It wasn't until the following June that I next visited the farm to see a sick cow and I saw Gyp – now fully grown – rocking along on a haycart.

I spotted him again at harvest-time, chasing rats among the stooks. He was always glad to see me, full of fun, bright-eyed and affectionate. But soundless.

There was a very long spell when none of Mr Wilkin's animals needed my help, and I did not see him or Gyp until I met them both at a sheepdog trial the following summer.

The huge field where the trial was being held was on the river's edge and the sunshine glinted on the water. The cars were drawn up along the side of the field, and groups of men, mainly competitors, stood around chatting as they watched the dogs working with the sheep. They were dressed in all sorts of clothing: cloth caps, trilbies, deer-stalkers or sometimes no hat at all; tweed jackets, best suits, open-necked shirts, fancy ties – and sometimes neither collar nor tie. Nearly all of them leaned on long crooks with the handles carved from rams' horns.

Their dogs, waiting their turn, were tied to the fence and it was wonderful to see the long row of waving tails and friendly expressions. Few of the dogs knew each other but there was not a single growl, never mind a fight.

I went over to Mr Wilkin who was leaning against his
car which was parked within sight of the final pen.
Gyp was tied to the bumper and was watching with
interest as each dog took its turn. Mrs Wilkin was
sitting on a camp stool by his side.

"Are you running a dog today, Mr Wilkin?" I asked.

"No, not this time. I've just come to watch," he
replied.

I had been there for about ten minutes when suddenly the farmer lifted a pointing finger. "Look who's there!"

George Crossley with Sweep were making their way to the starting post. Gyp suddenly stiffened and sat up very straight, one ear cocked, the other flat, making him look more lop-sided than ever.

It was over a year since he had seen his brother and it seemed unlikely, I thought, that he would remember him. But he was obviously *very* interested and, as the judge waved his white handkerchief to begin the trial and the three sheep were released from the far corner of the field, Gyp rose slowly to his feet.

A gesture from Mr Crossley sent Sweep racing round the edge of the field in a wide, joyous gallop, and as he neared the sheep a whistle from Mr Crossley made him drop onto his stomach. From then on, it was easy to see that Sweep was going to be a champion as he darted and crouched at his master's commands. Short whistles, long whistles; Sweep understood them all.

No other dog all day had brought his sheep through the three pairs of gates as easily as Sweep did now and as he neared the final pen, it was obvious he was going to win unless the sheep scattered at the last moment.

George Crossley opened the gate wide and held out his crook. I could hardly hear his commands to Sweep, but his quiet words brought the dog wriggling inch by inch over the grass towards the sheep. Were they going to go bounding away and spoil everything? I held my breath. But no, after hesitating and looking around a few times, the sheep turned and entered the pen and Mr Crossley banged the gate behind them.

As he did so, he turned to Sweep with a happy cry of "Good lad!" and the dog answered with a quick wag of his tail.

At that, Gyp, who had been standing very still, watching every move intently, raised his head and gave a single loud bark which echoed round the field.

"WOOF!" went Gyp and we all stared at him in astonishment.

"Did you hear that?" gasped Mrs Wilkin.

"Well, I don't believe it!" her husband burst out, looking open-mouthed at his dog.

Gyp didn't seem to realise that he had done anything unusual. George Crossley came over with Sweep and the two dogs greeted each other happily. Mr Wilkin let Gyp off his lead and within seconds the two dogs were rolling around, chewing playfully at each other as they used to do as pups.

I suppose the Wilkins, as well as myself, had the feeling that this event might encourage Gyp to bark like any other dog, but it was not to be.

Six years later I was at the farm and went to the house to get some hot water. As Mrs Wilkin handed me the bucket, she looked down at Gyp who was basking in the sunshine outside the kitchen door.

"There you are, you funny fellow," she said to the dog.

I laughed. "Has he ever barked since that day?"

Mrs Wilkin shook her head. "No, he hasn't, not a sound. I waited a long time but I don't think he'll ever bark."

"Ah well, it's not important. But I'll never forget that afternoon at the trial," I said.

"Nor will I!" Mrs Wilkin looked at Gyp again, and she smiled as she remembered. "Poor old lad. Eight years old and only one woof!"